Grade 4

Treasures

Teacher's Resource Book

Mc Graw Hill **Macmillan McGraw-Hill**

Photography Credits

B

The **McGraw·Hill** Companies

Macmillan
McGraw-Hill

Published by Macmillan/McGraw-Hill, of McGraw-Hill Education, a division of The McGraw-Hill Companies, Inc., Two Penn Plaza, New York, New York 10121.

Printed in the United States of America

3 4 5 6 7 8 9 10 021 11 10 09 08 07 06

Contents

Weekly Student Contracts

Helping Students Manage Their Time

Weekly Student Contracts help students manage their independent work time.

A Student Contract is supplied for each week of instruction in Treasures. The contract lists independent activities provided in the program that support priority skills for the week. The activities listed include:

- workstation activities
- leveled readers and activities
- technology activities
- practice book activities

Name _____ Date _____

My To-Do List
✔ Put a check next to the activities you complete.

📖 **Reading**
☐ Practice fluency
☐ Read a mystery story

🔤 **Word Study**
☐ Look up multiple-meaning words
☐ Rhyme words with short vowel sounds

✏️ **Writing**
☐ Write a paragraph
☐ Write a headline

🔬 **Science**
☐ Research mysteries in nature
☐ Create a poster

🌐 **Social Studies**
☐ Create a history game
☐ Play it with a partner

⚓ **Leveled Readers**
☐ Write About It!
☐ Content Connection

🖱️ **Technology**
☐ Vocabulary Puzzlemaker
☐ Fluency Solutions
☐ Listening Library
☐ www.macmillanmh.com

🖌️ **Independent Practice**
☐ Practice Book, 1–7
☐ Grammar Practice Book, 1–6
☐ Spelling Practice Book, 1–6

Contracts   Unit 1 • The Mystery of the Missing Lunch   ③

How to Use the Student Contract

- At the beginning of each week, distribute a contract to each student.

- Discuss with students each activity listed in the contract.

- Identify activities and practice book pages that you expect students to complete by the end of the week.

- As students complete each assigned activity, ask them to check off the completed task on the contract and store their work in a folder.

- Students can choose other activities from the contract after completing the assigned activities.

- Check the work in the folder at the end of each week. The folder can also be sent home for review.

My To-Do List

✔ Put a check next to the activities you complete.

📖 Reading

- ☐ Practice fluency
- ☐ Read a mystery story

🔤 Word Study

- ☐ Look up multiple-meaning words
- ☐ Rhyme words with short vowel sounds

✏️ Writing

- ☐ Write a paragraph
- ☐ Write a headline

🔍 Science

- ☐ Research mysteries in nature
- ☐ Create a poster

🌎 Social Studies

- ☐ Create a history game
- ☐ Play it with a partner

📖 Leveled Readers

- ☐ Write About It!
- ☐ Content Connection

🖱️ Technology

- ☐ Vocabulary Puzzlemaker
- ☐ Fluency Solutions
- ☐ Listening Library
- ☐ www.macmillanmh.com

📝 Independent Practice

- ☐ Practice Book, I–7
- ☐ Grammar Practice Book, I–6
- ☐ Spelling Practice Book, I–6

© Macmillan/McGraw-Hill

My To-Do List

✔ Put a check next to the activities you complete.

📖 Reading

- ☐ Practice fluency
- ☐ Choose a book to read

✏️ Writing

- ☐ Write a description
- ☐ Write a letter home

🌎 Social Studies

- ☐ Study a desert ecosystem
- ☐ Draw a desert and label it

🖱️ Technology

- ☐ Vocabulary Puzzlemaker
- ☐ Fluency Solutions
- ☐ Listening Library
- ☐ www.macmillanmh.com

Ⓐ Ⓑ Ⓒ Word Study

- ☐ Look up and define words
- ☐ Use words with long *a*

🔍 Science

- ☐ Research deserts
- ☐ Share true/false questions

📖 Leveled Readers

- ☐ Write About It!
- ☐ Content Connection

✏️ Independent Practice

- ☐ Practice Book, 8–14
- ☐ Grammar Practice Book, 7–12
- ☐ Spelling Practice Book, 7–12

My To-Do List

✔ **Put a check next to the activities you complete.**

📖 Reading

- ☐ Practice fluency
- ☐ Choose a story to read

Ⓐ Ⓑ Word Study

- ☐ Write compound words
- ☐ Use words with long e

✏️ Writing

- ☐ Write a book review
- ☐ Write a personal response

🔍 Science

- ☐ Write about trees
- ☐ Draw and label a tree

🌎 Social Studies

- ☐ Research jobs related to trees
- ☐ Research states that make paper

📖 Leveled Readers

- ☐ Write About It!
- ☐ Content Connection

🖱️ Technology

- ☐ Vocabulary Puzzlemaker
- ☐ Fluency Solutions
- ☐ Listening Library
- ☐ www.macmillanmh.com

📝 Independent Practice

- ☐ Practice Book, 15–21
- ☐ Grammar Practice Book, 13–18
- ☐ Spelling Practice Book, 13–18

My To-Do List

✔ **Put a check next to the activities you complete.**

Reading

- ☐ Practice fluency
- ☐ Read a story

(ABC) Word Study

- ☐ Look up pronunciations of words
- ☐ Use words with long *i*

Writing

- ☐ Write a personal letter
- ☐ Write a paragraph about your future career

Science

- ☐ Research the solar system
- ☐ Draw a diagram of the nine planets

Social Studies

- ☐ Write a list of rules
- ☐ Share your list with others

Leveled Readers

- ☐ Write About It!
- ☐ Content Connection

Technology

- ☐ Vocabulary Puzzlemaker
- ☐ Fluency Solutions
- ☐ Listening Library
- ☐ www.macmillanmh.com

Independent Practice

- ☐ Practice Book, 22–28
- ☐ Grammar Practice Book, 19–24
- ☐ Spelling Practice Book, 19–24

My To-Do List

✔ **Put a check next to the activities you complete.**

📖 Reading

☐ Practice fluency
☐ Choose a story to read

Ⓐ Ⓑ Ⓒ Word Study

☐ Play a word-card game
☐ Use words with long *o*

✏️ Writing

☐ Write a personal narrative
☐ Outline a magazine article

🔍 Science

☐ Research how to build a raft
☐ Illustrate your directions

🌎 Social Studies

☐ Study a river in your state
☐ Draw a map of it

📖 Leveled Readers

☐ Write About It!
☐ Content Connection

🖱️ Technology

☐ Vocabulary Puzzlemaker
☐ Fluency Solutions
☐ Listening Library
☐ www.macmillanmh.com

Independent Practice

☐ Practice Book, 29–35
☐ Grammar Practice Book, 25–30
☐ Spelling Practice Book, 25–30

My To-Do List

✔ Put a check next to the activities you complete.

📖 Reading

- ☐ Practice fluency
- ☐ Read a book or article

✏️ Writing

- ☐ Write a persuasive letter
- ☐ Write about team spirit

🌎 Social Studies

- ☐ Use an almanac
- ☐ Create a table

🖱️ Technology

- ☐ Vocabulary Puzzlemaker
- ☐ Fluency Solutions
- ☐ Listening Library
- ☐ www.macmillanmh.com

(ABC) Word Study

- ☐ Write using context clues
- ☐ Sort words with *ch* and *tch*

🔍 Science

- ☐ Research baseball pitches
- ☐ Draw and label a diagram

📖 Leveled Readers

- ☐ Write About It!
- ☐ Content Connection

🖌️ Independent Practice

- ☐ Practice Book, 38–44
- ☐ Grammar Practice Book, 33–38
- ☐ Spelling Practice Book, 33–38

My To-Do List

✔ Put a check next to the activities you complete.

 Reading

☐ Practice fluency

☐ Choose a story to read

 **Word Study**

☐ Look up word origins

☐ List words with digraphs *th*, *sh*, *wh*, *ph*

 Writing

☐ Write a letter to the editor

☐ Write a radio ad

 Science

☐ Research a type of rock

☐ Write a step-by-step guide

 Social Studies

☐ Write interview questions

☐ Role-play an interview

 Leveled Readers

☐ Write About It!

☐ Content Connection

 Technology

☐ Vocabulary Puzzlemaker

☐ Fluency Solutions

☐ Listening Library

☐ www.macmillanmh.com

Independent Practice

☐ Practice Book, 45–51

☐ Grammar Practice Book, 39–44

☐ Spelling Practice Book, 39–44

My To-Do List

✔ Put a check next to the activities you complete.

📕 Reading

- ☐ Practice fluency
- ☐ Read a magazine article

🅰🅱🅲 Word Study

- ☐ Use vocabulary words
- ☐ Sort words by consonant clusters

✏️ Writing

- ☐ Write a personal narrative
- ☐ Write a descriptive paragraph

🔍 Science

- ☐ Research the magnetic compass
- ☐ Describe using a compass

🌎 Social Studies

- ☐ Research different homes
- ☐ Share your writing

📖 Leveled Readers

- ☐ Write About It!
- ☐ Content Connection

🖱️ Technology

- ☐ Vocabulary Puzzlemaker
- ☐ Fluency Solutions
- ☐ Listening Library
- ☐ www.macmillanmh.com

Independent Practice

- ☐ Practice Book, 52–58
- ☐ Grammar Practice Book, 45–50
- ☐ Spelling Practice Book, 45–50

My To-Do List

✔ Put a check next to the activities you complete.

📖 Reading

- ☐ Practice fluency
- ☐ Read a biography

(ABC) Word Study

- ☐ Give clues about words
- ☐ Spell words with /är/ and /ôr/ sounds

✏ Writing

- ☐ Write a book review
- ☐ Write a moon poem

🔍 Science

- ☐ Research the light bulb
- ☐ Make a time line

🌎 Social Studies

- ☐ Research underground wiring
- ☐ Write a persuasive paragraph

📖 Leveled Readers

- ☐ Write About It!
- ☐ Content Connection

🖱 Technology

- ☐ Vocabulary Puzzlemaker
- ☐ Fluency Solutions
- ☐ Listening Library
- ☐ www.macmillanmh.com

🖌 Independent Practice

- ☐ Practice Book, 59–65
- ☐ Grammar Practice Book, 51–56
- ☐ Spelling Practice Book, 51–56

My To-Do List

✔ Put a check next to the activities you complete.

📖 Reading

☐ Practice fluency
☐ Read about unusual pets

🔤 Word Study

☐ Define vocabulary words
☐ Use words with *air, are, ear, ere*

✏️ Writing

☐ Write a letter to a librarian
☐ Write a persuasive paragraph about snakes

🔍 Science

☐ Research reptiles
☐ List local reptiles

🌎 Social Studies

☐ Research tropical rain forests
☐ Draw a rain-forest map

📖 Leveled Readers

☐ Write About It!
☐ Content Connection

🖱️ Technology

☐ Vocabulary Puzzlemaker
☐ Fluency Solutions
☐ Listening Library
☐ www.macmillanmh.com

Independent Practice

☐ Practice Book, 66–72
☐ Grammar Practice Book, 57–62
☐ Spelling Practice Book, 57–62

My To-Do List

✔ **Put a check next to the activities you complete.**

 ## Reading

☐ Practice fluency

☐ Choose a folk tale

 ## Word Study

☐ Look up synonyms

☐ Spell words with /ûr/

 ## Writing

☐ Write using dialogue

☐ Write directions for playing a game

 ## Science

☐ Research the coyote

☐ Write about the coyote

 ## Social Studies

☐ Find where coyotes live

☐ Draw a coyote map

 ## Leveled Readers

☐ Write About It!

☐ Content Connection

 ## Technology

☐ Vocabulary Puzzlemaker

☐ Fluency Solutions

☐ Listening Library

☐ www.macmillanmh.com

Independent Practice

☐ Practice Book, 75–81

☐ Grammar Practice Book, 65–70

☐ Spelling Practice Book, 65–70

My To-Do List

✔ Put a check next to the activities you complete.

📖 Reading

☐ Practice fluency
☐ Read a biography

ⒶⒷⒸ Word Study

☐ Build words with prefixes
☐ Use words with silent consonants

✏️ Writing

☐ Write a poem
☐ Write about someone who inspires you

🔍 Science

☐ Research the North Star
☐ Write a letter about the North Star

🌎 Social Studies

☐ Study facts about the Underground Railroad
☐ Write a journal entry

📖 Leveled Readers

☐ Write About It!
☐ Content Connection

🖱️ Technology

☐ Vocabulary Puzzlemaker
☐ Fluency Solutions
☐ Listening Library
☐ www.macmillanmh.com

🖌️ Independent Practice

☐ Practice Book, 82–88
☐ Grammar Practice Book, 71–76
☐ Spelling Practice Book, 71–76

My To-Do List

✔ Put a check next to the activities you complete.

 Reading

☐ Practice fluency

☐ Choose two articles to read

 Word Study

☐ Build words using -ed and -ing

☐ Use words with soft c and g sounds

 Writing

☐ Write a persuasive letter

☐ Conduct an interview

 Science

☐ Research safe cleaners

☐ Write directions

Social Studies

☐ Read a magazine article

☐ Write a summary

 Leveled Readers

☐ Write About It!

☐ Content Connection

 Technology

☐ Vocabulary Puzzlemaker

☐ Fluency Solutions

☐ Listening Library

☐ www.macmillanmh.com

 Independent Practice

☐ Practice Book, 89–95

☐ Grammar Practice Book, 77–82

☐ Spelling Practice Book, 77–82

My To-Do List

✔ **Put a check next to the activities you complete.**

Reading
- [ ] Practice fluency
- [ ] Read a legend

Word Study
- [ ] Look up and illustrate homophones
- [ ] Work with plural words

Writing
- [ ] Write a play
- [ ] Write a descriptive paragraph

Science
- [ ] Study types of chili peppers
- [ ] Create a recipe card

Social Studies
- [ ] Research Native American tribes and celebrations
- [ ] Use a Venn Diagram

Leveled Readers
- [ ] Write About It!
- [ ] Content Connection

Technology
- [ ] Vocabulary Puzzlemaker
- [ ] Fluency Solutions
- [ ] Listening Library
- [ ] www.macmillanmh.com

Independent Practice
- [ ] Practice Book, 96–102
- [ ] Grammar Practice Book, 83–88
- [ ] Spelling Practice Book, 83–88

Name _____   Date _____

My To-Do List

✔ Put a check next to the activities you complete.

📖 Reading

☐ Practice fluency
☐ Read a biography

Ⓐ Word Study

☐ Look up and illustrate multiple-meaning words
☐ Write compound words

✏️ Writing

☐ Write a character sketch
☐ Write interview questions

🔍 Science

☐ Study facts about snow
☐ Write a snow poem

🌎 Social Studies

☐ Research rain and snowfall in your state
☐ Describe your state's climate

📖 Leveled Readers

☐ Write About It!
☐ Content Connection

🖱️ Technology

☐ Vocabulary Puzzlemaker
☐ Fluency Solutions
☐ Listening Library
☐ www.macmillanmh.com

🖌️ Independent Practice

☐ Practice Book, 103–109
☐ Grammar Practice Book, 89–94
☐ Spelling Practice Book, 89–94

My To-Do List

✔ Put a check next to the activities you complete.

📖 Reading

☐ Practice fluency

☐ Choose a story to read

Ⓐ Ⓑ Word Study

☐ Write meanings of words with prefix *mis-*

☐ Sort words and add endings

✏️ Writing

☐ Write an explanation

☐ Write about taking care of pets

🔍 Science

☐ Research how dogs help people

☐ Create an illustrated poster

🌎 Social Studies

☐ Research animal shelters

☐ Graph numbers of pet adopted

📖 Leveled Readers

☐ Write About It!

☐ Content Connection

🖱️ Technology

☐ Vocabulary Puzzlemaker

☐ Fluency Solutions

☐ Listening Library

☐ www.macmillanmh.com

🖌️ Independent Practice

☐ Practice Book, 112–118

☐ Grammar Practice Book, 97–102

☐ Spelling Practice Book, 97–102

Contracts

My To-Do List

✔ Put a check next to the activities you complete.

 Reading

☐ Practice fluency

☐ Choose a story to read

 Word Study

☐ Use words from same family

☐ Add endings -es, -ed, -er, -est, -ly

 Writing

☐ Write step-by-step instructions

☐ Write about an invention

 Science

☐ Research inventions

☐ Make a glossary of terms

Social Studies

☐ Research computers

☐ Write a paragraph about computers

 Leveled Readers

☐ Write About It!

☐ Content Connection

 Technology

☐ Vocabulary Puzzlemaker

☐ Fluency Solutions

☐ Listening Library

☐ www.macmillanmh.com

 Independent Practice

☐ Practice Book, 119–125

☐ Grammar Practice Book, 103–108

☐ Spelling Practice Book, 103–108

My To-Do List

✔ Put a check next to the activities you complete.

Reading

- [ ] Practice fluency
- [ ] Choose an article to read

Word Study

- [ ] Write sentences with context clues
- [ ] Sort words by vowel spellings

Writing

- [ ] Write a fictional narrative
- [ ] Write about saving energy

Science

- [ ] Research wind farms
- [ ] Write a report

Social Studies

- [ ] Research first uses of electricity
- [ ] Write a short report

Leveled Readers

- [ ] Write About It!
- [ ] Content Connection

Technology

- [ ] Vocabulary Puzzlemaker
- [ ] Fluency Solutions
- [ ] Listening Library
- [ ] www.macmillanmh.com

Independent Practice

- [ ] Practice Book, 126–132
- [ ] Grammar Practice Book, 109–114
- [ ] Spelling Practice Book, 109–114

Contracts

My To-Do List

✔ **Put a check next to the activities you complete.**

📖 Reading

☐ Practice fluency

☐ Choose a nonfiction article or book to read

Ⓐ Word Study

☐ Use homographs in sentences

☐ Sort words by vowel sounds /ou/ and /oi/

✏️ Writing

☐ Write a statement of opinion

☐ Write a paragraph

🔍 Science

☐ Research facts about whales

☐ Write a rhyming poem

🌎 Social Studies

☐ Research animal photographers

☐ Illustrate an animal

📖 Leveled Readers

☐ Write About It!

☐ Content Connection

🖱 Technology

☐ Vocabulary Puzzlemaker

☐ Fluency Solutions

☐ Listening Library

☐ www.macmillanmh.com

✒️ Independent Practice

☐ Practice Book, 133–139

☐ Grammar Practice Book, 115–120

☐ Spelling Practice Book, 115–120

My To-Do List

✔ Put a check next to the activities you complete.

📕 Reading

☐ Practice fluency

☐ Choose a nonfiction book to read

(ABC) Word Study

☐ Write context clues in sentences

☐ Sort words by three spelling patterns

✏️ Writing

☐ Write about a mural

☐ Write a how-to paragraph

🔍 Science

☐ Research coral reefs

☐ Compare and contrast reefs

🌎 Social Studies

☐ Research Atlantis

☐ Write an example of hyperbole

📖 Leveled Readers

☐ Write About It!

☐ Content Connection

🖱️ Technology

☐ Vocabulary Puzzlemaker

☐ Fluency Solutions

☐ Listening Library

☐ www.macmillanmh.com

📝 Independent Practice

☐ Practice Book, 140–146

☐ Grammar Practice Book, 121–126

☐ Spelling Practice Book, 121–126

My To-Do List

✔ Put a check next to the activities you complete.

 ## Reading

- [ ] Practice fluency
- [ ] Choose a book to read

 ## Word Study

- [ ] Work with connotations and denotations
- [ ] Play a syllable game

 ## Writing

- [ ] List likeness and differences
- [ ] Write a poem about friendship

 ## Science

- [ ] Research popcorn facts
- [ ] Diagram how popcorn pops

 ## Social Studies

- [ ] Research popcorn history
- [ ] Survey classmates

 ## Leveled Readers

- [ ] Write About It!
- [ ] Content Connection

Technology

- [ ] Vocabulary Puzzlemaker
- [ ] Fluency Solutions
- [ ] Listening Library
- [ ] www.macmillanmh.com

 ## Independent Practice

- [ ] Practice Book, 149–155
- [ ] Grammar Practice Book, 129–134
- [ ] Spelling Practice Book, 129–134

My To-Do List

✔ Put a check next to the activities you complete.

Reading

- [ ] Practice fluency
- [ ] Read a play

Word Study

- [ ] Write antonyms
- [ ] Sort words by VCV syllables

Writing

- [ ] Advertise a play
- [ ] Write dialogue

Science

- [ ] Research joints
- [ ] Diagram the knee or elbow joint

Social Studies

- [ ] List interview questions
- [ ] Role-play the interview

Leveled Readers

- [ ] Write About It!
- [ ] Content Connection

Technology

- [ ] Vocabulary Puzzlemaker
- [ ] Fluency Solutions
- [ ] Listening Library
- [ ] www.macmillanmh.com

Independent Practice

- [ ] Practice Book, 156–162
- [ ] Grammar Practice Book, 135–140
- [ ] Spelling Practice Book, 135–140

My To-Do List

✔ Put a check next to the activities you complete.

📕 Reading

- ☐ Practice fluency
- ☐ Read a magazine article

Ⓐ Ⓑ Ⓒ Word Study

- ☐ Complete several analogies
- ☐ Sort words by context clues

✏️ Writing

- ☐ Write a brief summary
- ☐ Write a concrete poem

🔍 Science

- ☐ Research jellyfish
- ☐ Diagram a jellyfish

🌎 Social Studies

- ☐ Research a Spanish explorer
- ☐ Map the explorer's route

Leveled Readers

- ☐ Write About It!
- ☐ Content Connection

🖱️ Technology

- ☐ Vocabulary Puzzlemaker
- ☐ Fluency Solutions
- ☐ Listening Library
- ☐ www.macmillanmh.com

Independent Practice

- ☐ Practice Book, 163–169
- ☐ Grammar Practice Book, 141–146
- ☐ Spelling Practice Book, 141–146

Name _____ Date _____

My To-Do List

✔ Put a check next to the activities you complete.

Reading
- ☐ Practice fluency
- ☐ Choose a story

Word Study
- ☐ Use context clues
- ☐ List words with schwa + *r*

Writing
- ☐ Write an introduction
- ☐ Describe a favorite painting

Science
- ☐ Make a color wheel
- ☐ Write how to mix colors

Social Studies
- ☐ Research a monument
- ☐ Write a description

Leveled Readers
- ☐ Write About It!
- ☐ Content Connection

Technology
- ☐ Vocabulary Puzzlemaker
- ☐ Fluency Solutions
- ☐ Listening Library
- ☐ www.macmillanmh.com

Independent Practice
- ☐ Practice Book, 170–176
- ☐ Grammar Practice Book, 147–152
- ☐ Spelling Practice Book, 147–152

Name _____ Date _____

My To-Do List

✔ Put a check next to the activities you complete.

Reading

- ☐ Practice fluency
- ☐ Choose a tall tale to read

Word Study

- ☐ Use context clues
- ☐ List words with schwa + l

Writing

- ☐ Write a character description
- ☐ Write a journal entry

Science

- ☐ Research a horse breed
- ☐ Write an article about it

Social Studies

- ☐ Look up horse facts
- ☐ Make a horse time line

Leveled Readers

- ☐ Write About It!
- ☐ Content Connection

Technology

- ☐ Vocabulary Puzzlemaker
- ☐ Fluency Solutions
- ☐ Listening Library
- ☐ www.macmillanmh.com

Independent Practice

- ☐ Practice Book, 177–183
- ☐ Grammar Practice Book, 153–158
- ☐ Spelling Practice Book, 153–158

My To-Do List

✔ Put a check next to the activities you complete.

Reading

☐ Practice fluency
☐ Read a science fiction story

ABC Word Study

☐ Look up story words
☐ List words with schwa + *n*

Writing

☐ List details of a place
☐ Write interview questions

Science

☐ Find facts about gold
☐ Write True/False questions

Social Studies

☐ Research the Gold Rush
☐ Create a time line

Leveled Readers

☐ Write About It!
☐ Content Connection

Technology

☐ Vocabulary Puzzlemaker
☐ Fluency Solutions
☐ Listening Library
☐ www.macmillanmh.com

Independent Practice

☐ Practice Book, 186–192
☐ Grammar Practice Book, 161–166
☐ Spelling Practice Book, 161–166

Contracts

Name _____   Date _____

My To-Do List

✔ **Put a check next to the activities you complete.**

 Reading

☐ Practice fluency

☐ Choose a fantasy story to read

 Word Study

☐ Look up related words

☐ Work with homophones

 Writing

☐ Write questions and answers

☐ Write a descriptive paragraph

 Science

☐ Research an endangered animal

☐ Create an advertisement

 Social Studies

☐ Research animals as symbols

☐ Create an animal poster

 Leveled Readers

☐ Write About It!

☐ Content Connection

 Technology

☐ Vocabulary Puzzlemaker

☐ Fluency Solutions

☐ Listening Library

☐ www.macmillanmh.com

Independent Practice

☐ Practice Book, 193–199

☐ Grammar Practice Book, 167–172

☐ Spelling Practice Book, 167–172

My To-Do List

✔ Put a check next to the activities you complete.

📕 Reading

- ☐ Practice fluency
- ☐ Read a nonfiction article

Ⓐ Word Study

- ☐ Work on pronunciation
- ☐ Use words with prefixes

✏️ Writing

- ☐ Write a personal essay
- ☐ Write about current events

🔍 Science

- ☐ Research tree parts
- ☐ Draw a diagram of a tree and add labels

🌎 Social Studies

- ☐ Research local trees
- ☐ Write a persuasive paragraph

📖 Leveled Readers

- ☐ Write About It!
- ☐ Content Connection

🖱️ Technology

- ☐ Vocabulary Puzzlemaker
- ☐ Fluency Solutions
- ☐ Listening Library
- ☐ www.macmillanmh.com

📝 Independent Practice

- ☐ Practice Book, 200–206
- ☐ Grammar Practice Book, 173–178
- ☐ Spelling Practice Book, 173–178

My To-Do List

✔ **Put a check next to the activities you complete.**

 Reading

☐ Practice fluency
☐ Read a biography

 **Word Study**

☐ Rewrite sentences with *-ed*
☐ Use words with suffixes

Writing

☐ List ideas about a job
☐ Write interview questions

 Science

☐ Research a landform
☐ Draw a diagram of it

 Social Studies

☐ Research a national monument or statue
☐ Draw and caption it

 Leveled Readers

☐ Write About It!
☐ Content Connection

Technology

☐ Vocabulary Puzzlemaker
☐ Fluency Solutions
☐ Listening Library
☐ www.macmillanmh.com

Independent Practice

☐ Practice Book, 207–213
☐ Grammar Practice Book, 179–184
☐ Spelling Practice Book, 179–184

My To-Do List

✔ Put a check next to the activities you complete.

Reading

- [ ] Practice fluency
- [ ] Read a book about a place

Word Study

- [ ] Work with Greek prefixes
- [ ] Use words with the /er/ sound

Writing

- [ ] Write a summary
- [ ] Write about a sky object

Science

- [ ] List tips for staying healthy
- [ ] Illustrate a poster

Social Studies

- [ ] Research a person from history
- [ ] Write the person's story

Leveled Readers

- [ ] Write About It!
- [ ] Content Connection

Technology

- [ ] Vocabulary Puzzlemaker
- [ ] Fluency Solutions
- [ ] Listening Library
- [ ] www.macmillanmh.com

Independent Practice

- [ ] Practice Book, 214–220
- [ ] Grammar Practice Book, 185–190
- [ ] Spelling Practice Book, 185–190

Foldables™

by Dinah Zike

What are Foldables™?

Foldables are multi-dimensional graphic organizers that can be used for skills reinforcement, practice, and/or information organizing.

Why use Foldables™?

Not only do Foldables reinforce skills and strategies essential for reading success, they provide a kinesthetic tool for organizing and analyzing learning.

Dear Teacher,

A Foldable is a three-dimensional, student-made (and/or teacher-made) interactive graphic organizer based upon a skill. Making a Foldable gives students a fast, kinesthetic activity that helps them organize and retain information either before, during, or after reading. In this section of the *Teacher's Resource Book*, you will find instructions for making Foldables, as well as ideas on how to use them to reinforce and practice phonics, vocabulary, spelling, and comprehension skills.

In this section, you will find Foldables to help you

- replace photocopied activity sheets with student-generated print
- present content and skills in a clear, visual, kinesthetic format
- incorporate the use of such skills as comparing and contrasting, recognizing cause and effect, and finding similarities and differences
- assess student progress and learning levels
- immerse students in new and previously learned vocabulary and reading skills
- teach students unique ways to make study guides and practice materials, and
- provide students with a sense of ownership in their learning.

I am excited to hand these Foldable ideas and activities over to you and your students. Have fun using, adding to, and amending them to meet individual needs.

Sincerely,

Creating and Storing Foldables™

As you use the Foldables outlined in this *Teacher's Resource Book*, discuss with students how they can adapt them to make their own Foldable learning and study aids. Teach students to write—titles, vocabulary words, concepts, skills, questions, main ideas—on the front tabs of their Foldables. By doing this, key concepts are viewed every time a student looks at a Foldable. Foldables help students focus on and remember the information presented without being distracted by other print. Remind students to write more specific information—supporting ideas, examples of a concept, definitions, answers to questions, observations—under the tabs.

Turn one-gallon freezer bags into student portfolios and storage containers for Foldables.

 Cut the bottom corners off each bag so they won't hold air and will stack and store easily.

 Write student names across the top of the plastic portfolios with a permanent marker and cover the writing with two-inch clear tape to keep it from wearing off.

 Place a piece of cardboard inside each portfolio to give it strength and to act as a divider.

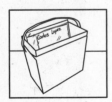 Store Foldables in a giant laundry soap box. Or, students can carry their portfolios in a three-ring binder if you place a strip of two-inch clear tape along one side and punch three holes through the taped edge.

Foldables

Foldables™
in this section

Basic Shapes

by Dinah Zike

These figures illustrate the basic folds that are referred to throughout the following section of this book.

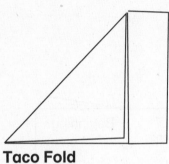

Taco Fold

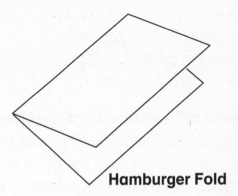

Hamburger Fold

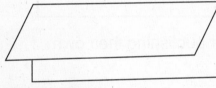

Hot Dog Fold

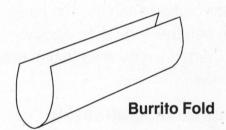

Burrito Fold

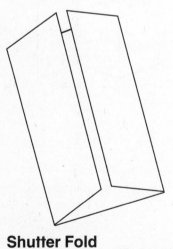

Shutter Fold

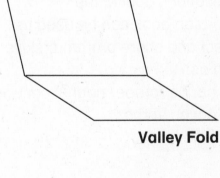

Valley Fold

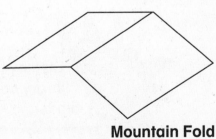

Mountain Fold

Foldables

Using the Accordion Book Foldable™
by Dinah Zike

Vocabulary and Vocabulary Strategy Applications
Use this Foldable to create vocabulary books that record examples and explanations on topics such as:
- word parts
- prefixes and suffixes
- using context clues
- using a dictionary

Comprehension Application
This Foldable is perfect for post-reading skills application. Use the book to record text sequence (first, next, last) or plot sequence (beginning, middle, end). Try color-coding each section so students can see the sequence clearly.

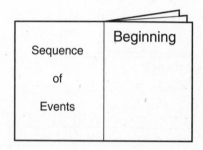

Students may wish to use this Foldable for publishing their own stories.

Grammar Application
Like the vocabulary strategy applications above, the accordion book can be used to collect and share grammar skills such as:

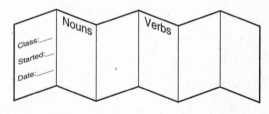

- nouns (proper nouns, common nouns)
- action verbs
- adjectives

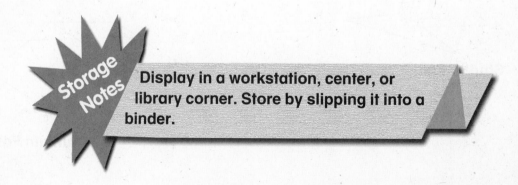

Storage Notes

Display in a workstation, center, or library corner. Store by slipping it into a binder.

Accordion Book Foldable™ Directions
by Dinah Zike

Materials:
- several sheets of 11" × 17" paper
- glue

Directions:

1. Fold each sheet of paper like a hamburger, but fold one side half an inch shorter than the other side. This will form a tab that is half an inch long.

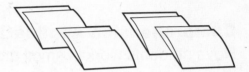

---

2. Fold this tab forward over the shorter side, then fold it back away from the shorter piece of paper. (In other words, fold it the opposite way.)

---

3. To form an accordion, glue a straight edge of one section into the valley of another section's tab.

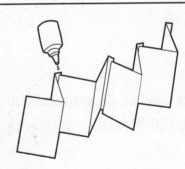

Tips! *Before gluing, stand the sections on end to form an accordion. This will help you see how to glue the sections together. Use different colors of paper to indicate sections of the book. Always place the extra tab at the back of the book so you can add more pages later.*

Foldables

Using the Standing Cube Foldable™
by Dinah Zike

Vocabulary Application
Use the Foldable for developing vocabulary concepts with students. Each side of the cube can show information about a word, such as its definition, example sentences, an illustration, and so on.

Comprehension Application
Have students work in small groups to create a Foldable about a story character they are studying. Each side of the Foldable should illustrate or tell about character traits.

Grammar Application
Use the Foldable to collect and share types of nouns or adjectives.

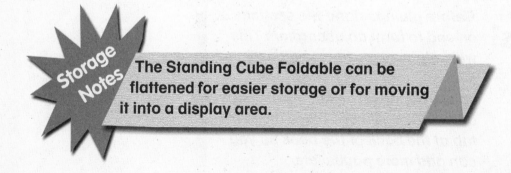

Storage Notes The Standing Cube Foldable can be flattened for easier storage or for moving it into a display area.

Standing Cube Foldable™ Directions
by Dinah Zike

Materials:
- two sheets of 11″ × 17″ paper
- glue

Directions:

1. Fold each sheet like a hamburger, but fold one side one-half inch shorter than the other side.

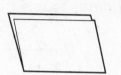

---

2. Fold the long side over the short side on both sheets of paper, making tabs.

---

3. On one of the folded papers, place a small amount of glue along the tab, next to the valley but not in it.

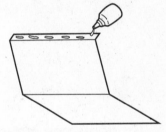

---

4. Place the non-folded edge of the second sheet of paper square into the valley and fold the glue-covered tab over this sheet of paper. Press flat until the glue holds. Repeat with the other side.

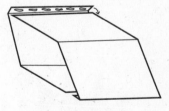

---

5. Allow the glue to dry completely before continuing. After the glue has dried, collapse the cube flat to write or draw on each side.

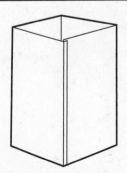

Foldables

Using the Large Word Study Book Foldable™
by Dinah Zike

Vocabulary and Phonics/Spelling Applications
With a small group, make a Foldable for vocabulary word study/review. Display the book in a workstation for repeated review. The size and the format also make it easy for you and students to use them as lap flashcards.

experiment

a test to see how something works

The scientist did an experiment to see what kind of food mice prefer.

Students can make individual books using this Foldable.

Storage Notes Collect and use these books through the year. Store each large book in a labeled legal-size folder.

Large Word Study Book Foldable™ Directions
by Dinah Zike

Materials:
- several sheets of 11" × 17" paper (one sheet for each word studied)
- stapler

Directions:

1. Fold each sheet like a hot dog, but fold one side one inch shorter than the other side.

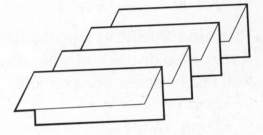

2. Stack the sheets so the folds are side by side.

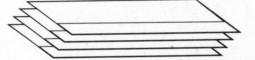

3. Staple sheets together along the tabbed end (the bottom of the pages).

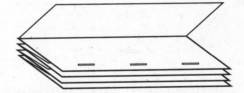

You can make a large word study book as an aid for vocabulary or spelling word lists. On the front of each tab, write a vocabulary or spelling word. Open the tab and write the definition and a sample sentence.

Use this Foldable to _____

_____

_____

Foldables

Using the Layered Book Foldable™
by Dinah Zike

Vocabulary Application
Have students create this Foldable to help them review vocabulary words. Have them write a word on each tab and then flip the tab to write the definition. The same thing can be done with antonyms and synonyms.

Phonics/Spelling Application
A review/study guide of letter sounds and word parts can be done with this Foldable. For example:
- Short vowels
- Long vowels
- Prefixes and suffixes
- Base words

Base Words
strong
fast
high
small

Comprehension Application
Use the Foldable to aid in the following skills reinforcement:
- Character study (one tab per story character)
- Summarize
- Generating Questions

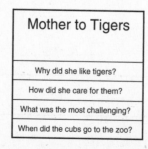

Mother to Tigers
Why did she like tigers?
How did she care for them?
What was the most challenging?
When did the cubs go to the zoo?

Study Skills and Grammar Applications
This Foldable can be used to review/reinforce concepts studied.

Layered Book Foldable™ Directions

by Dinah Zike

Materials:
- two sheets of 8½″ × 11″ paper
- glue

Directions:

1. Stack two sheets of paper so that the back sheet is one inch higher than the front sheet.

_____

2. Bring the bottom of both sheets upward and align the edges so that all of the layers or tabs are the same distance apart.

_____

3. When all tabs are an equal distance apart, fold the papers and crease well.

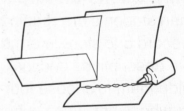

_____

4. Open the papers and glue them together along the valley, or inner center fold, or staple them along the mountain.

> **Tip!** *If you need more layers, use additional sheets of paper. Make the tabs smaller than one inch.*

Use this Foldable to _____

Foldables

Using the Four-Door Foldable™
by Dinah Zike

Grammar Application

Use this Foldable for information occurring in four categories. Have students create study guides and review grammar concepts such as four types of sentences. They may label each door with a type of sentence, then define each type and provide an example inside each door.

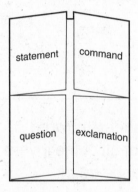

Comprehension Application

When students are reading a selection, they can use this Foldable to record and store information for summarizing. Have students write descriptions and include illustrations inside the four doors. Guide them to choose four categories of information. For example:
- who, what, when, where
- what, where, when, why/how
- character, plot, setting, conflict and resolution

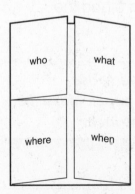

Foldables

Four-Door Foldable™ Directions

by Dinah Zike

Materials:
- sheet of 11″ × 17″ paper
- scissors

Directions:

1. Make a shutter fold.

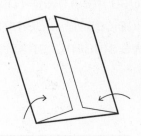

2. Fold the shutter fold in half like a hamburger. Crease well.

3. Open the folds and cut along the inside valley fold lines.

4. These cuts will form four doors on the inside of the book.

Use this Foldable to _____

_____

_____

_____

_____

Using the Two- and Three-Tab Foldable™
by Dinah Zike

Phonics/Spelling Application

Several options adapt this Foldable for prefix, base word, suffix study, and practice.

Use the Three-Tab Foldable to help students with word parts and syllabication. Open the tabs and write a base word in the center. Have students practice decoding words.

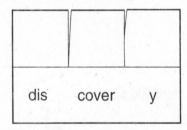

Another option is to cut only one of the valleys (see p. 50) so that the Foldable has two tabs of unequal size. Open the two tabs and write a base word on the bottom paper so that one word part is shown in each box. For further practice with pronunciation and word identification, fold the tabs over to make another word.

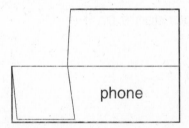

A third option is to make a two-tab variation. Use it to compare two different phonic/spelling elements such as soft *c* and hard *c*, vowel spellings, or word parts.

Directions and diagrams appear on page 50.

Foldables

Using the Two- and Three-Tab Foldables™ *continued*
by Dinah Zike

Comprehension Application

Use large poster board and choose a vertical or horizontal orientation to adapt the Three-Tab Foldable. Use it to create the following graphic organizers:

• Venn Diagram

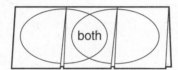

• Story Map

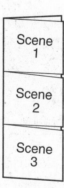

• K-W-L Chart

• Nonfiction text organizer

Directions and diagrams appear on page 50.

Foldables

Two- and Three-Tab Foldables™ Directions
by Dinah Zike

Materials:
- one 8½" × 11" sheet of paper or large poster board
- scissors

Directions:

1. Fold the sheet like a hot dog.

2. With the paper horizontal and the fold of the hot dog at the top, fold the right side toward the center to cover one half of the paper.

3. Fold the left side over the right side to make three sections.

4. Open the right and left folds. Place one hand between the two thicknesses of paper and cut up the two valleys so there are three tabs.

Options:
- Cut only one of the valleys so the Foldable has two tabs of unequal size.
- Use large poster board to make a Foldable on which you can record more information.

Use this Foldable to _____

_____

Using the Four- and Eight-Tab Foldable™
by Dinah Zike

Phonics/Spelling Application

Adapt the Four-Tab Foldable to review digraphs, blends, and vowel variant letter-sounds. Open the tabs and write a CVCe word on the bottom paper so that one letter is shown in each box. Have students practice identifying words.

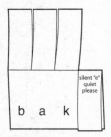

Another option is to make the Foldable with three tabs. At step 3 (see page 53), cut only the first and the third creases so that the middle tab is twice the size of the other two tabs. Open all three tabs and write a CVVC word on the bottom paper so that one letter is shown in each box and so that the middle two letters will be hidden by the middle tab.

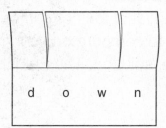

Or, cut only the first and second tabs and write a word that ends with double letters.

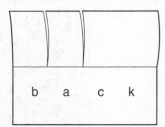

Directions and diagrams appear on page 53.

Foldables

Using the Four- and Eight-Tab Foldable™ *continued*
by Dinah Zike

Vocabulary and Phonics/Spelling Applications
Use the Eight-Tab Foldable to study and review spelling or vocabulary words. For instance, have students do a cumulative study of one of the following:
- phonic elements such as blends and digraphs
- suffixes and prefixes

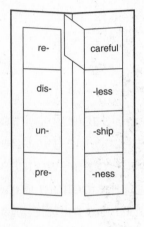

Comprehension Application
The Eight-Tab Foldable is an ideal tool for comparing two texts. Have students use the tabs to compare and contrast four elements: characters, setting, problem, solution. The Foldable is also helpful for summarizing nonfiction.

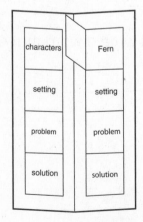
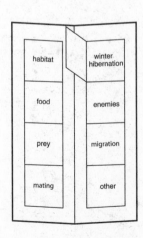

Four- and Eight-Tab Foldable™ Directions

by Dinah Zike

Materials:

- one 8½″ × 11″ sheet of paper
- scissors

add these for the Eight-Tab Foldable:

- another 8½″ × 11″ sheet of paper
- one large sheet of construction paper
- glue

Directions:

1. Fold a sheet of paper into a hot dog.

2. With the paper horizontal and the fold of the hot dog at the top, fold the hot dog into four vertical sections.

3. Open these folds. Place one hand between the folded hot dog and cut up the three fold lines so there are four tabs.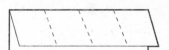

4. To make the Eight-Tab Foldable, follow steps 1–3 with a second sheet of paper. Then fold the construction paper like a hot dog. Open the construction paper. Glue the tabbed hot dogs to the inside so they open like the pages of a book.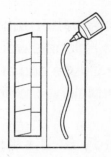

Use this Foldable to _____

_____

Foldables

Using the Matchbook Foldable™ and Portfolio
by Dinah Zike

Vocabulary Application

With students create Foldables for weekly vocabulary. Write the vocabulary word on the front. Have students write a sentence for the inside.

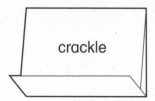

Phonics/Spelling Application

Use the Foldable for review of phonics and/or spelling words.

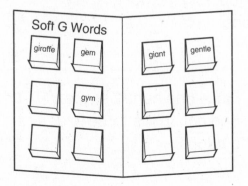

Comprehension Application

This Foldable works for reinforcing skills such as:
- Cause and effect
- Making predictions

Study Skills Application

If students are studying a list such as state capitals or even multiplication tables, the portfolio is a great small group or whole class review tool.

Matchbook Foldable™ and Portfolio Directions

by Dinah Zike

Materials:
- several sheets of 8½″ × 11″ paper
- poster board
- scissors
- glue

Directions:

1. Fold each sheet like a hamburger, but fold it so that one side is one inch longer than the other side.

2. Fold the one-inch tab over the short side to form an envelope-like fold.

3. Fold each hamburger in half. Cut along the fold line.

4. Fold the poster board like a hamburger.

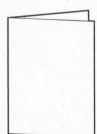

5. Use the small hamburgers to record information. Glue them onto the inside of the poster board.

Using the Shutter Foldable™
by Dinah Zike

Comprehension Application

There are many ways to use the Shutter Foldable to review and study comprehension skills. Larger paper can be used so that a small group or a class can create one of these for literacy study. Consider having students retell or summarize the story on the middle inside panel. Then have them use the outer panels to analyze the following:

- Facts and Opinions (for nonfiction)
- Cause and Effect
- Before and After
- Fantasy and Reality
- Pros and Cons (for persuasion)
- Problem and Solution
- Compare and Contrast

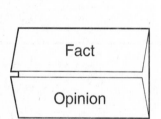

Storage Notes Large Shutter Foldables can be stored in an empty (and clean!) pizza box.

Shutter Foldable™ Directions

by Dinah Zike

Materials:

- 8½″ × 11″ paper

Directions:

1. Begin as if you are going to make a hamburger fold, but instead of folding the paper, pinch it to show the midpoint.

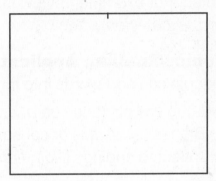

2. Open the sheet. Fold both of the outside edges in to touch the middle mark.

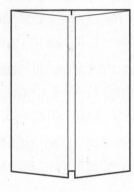

Use this Foldable to _____

_____

_____

_____

_____

Foldables

Using the Pyramid Foldable™
by Dinah Zike

Use this Foldable with data occurring in threes.

Vocabulary Application
The Pyramid Foldable can be used to sort and review concepts studied. For example, review three different inflectional endings (-*tion*, -*sion*, -*cion*).

Phonics/Spelling Application
Students can sort words into three categories. Some examples:

- Long vowels (such as *o_e, oa, o*)
- Blends (*sl, st, sw*) or consonant digraphs
- Inflected endings (-*ial, -tion, -ious*)

Comprehension Application
Not only can students use the pyramid to record information about what they read, they can do it in a few different ways. With one pyramid they can do things such as the following:

- Compare three different story characters
- Create a K-W-L chart
- Record information about story beginning, middle, and end

Students can glue together three pyramids to create small dioramas depicting scenes (from fiction) and concepts (from nonfiction).

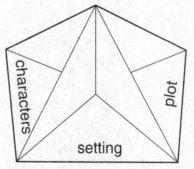

Storage Notes
Several pyramids can be strung together and hung from the ceiling for a vertical display.

Pyramid Foldable™ Directions
by Dinah Zike

Materials:
- one 8½″ × 11″ sheet of paper
- scissors
- glue

Directions:

1. Fold the sheet into a taco. Cut off the excess rectangular tab formed by the fold.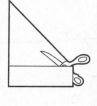

2. Open the folded taco and refold it like a taco the opposite way to create an X-fold.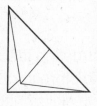

3. Cut one of the valleys to the center of the X, or the midpoint, and stop. This forms two triangular flaps.

4. Glue one of the flaps under the other, forming a pyramid.

Use this Foldable to _____

_____

_____

_____

_____

_____

_____

Using the Two- or Three-Pocket Foldable™
by Dinah Zike

Vocabulary and Phonics/Spelling Applications

Have students use this Foldable as a study aid. As they learn words, students may sort and store copies of Spelling Word Cards or Vocabulary Word Cards (see pages 66–95 and 96–125 in this book) in the pockets of this Foldable. Have students label the pockets as shown below. As they study the words, have them move the cards to the appropriate pockets.

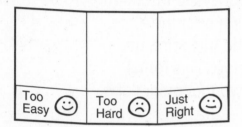 

Comprehension Application

When students are comparing and contrasting ideas in a selection, they can use this Foldable to record and store information for retelling or summarizing. This works with skills such as:

- Fact and opinion
- Make and confirm predictions
- Cause and Effect
- K-W-L

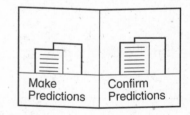

Tip! *Send this Foldable home with students so they can review and sort words with family members.*

Storage Notes Heavy stock paper will improve durability. Post the Foldable on a bulletin board for use during workstation time.

Two- or Three-Pocket Foldable™ Directions

by Dinah Zike

Materials:
- one 11" × 17" sheet of paper
- glue

Directions:

1. Begin as if you are going to make a hot dog, but fold over only about three inches.

2. Fold the right side toward the center, then fold the left side over the right side to make three sections. (Or, fold in half to make two pockets.)

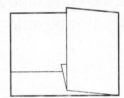

3. Glue the right and left edges of the original fold so that three pockets are created.

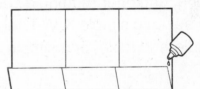

Use this Foldable to _____

_____

_____

_____

_____

Foldables

Using Folded Tables and Charts
by Dinah Zike

Depending upon the amount of data, the table or chart can be adapted and reformatted.

Vocabulary and Phonics/Spelling Applications
Have students use this Foldable as a study aid. Have them sort the words into categories and write them in the appropriate columns.

Vocabulary Strategies Application
Students can study words that have:
- prefixes and suffixes
- more than one meaning
- synonyms and antonyms

Multiple Meaning Words		
Word	Definition	Definition

Comprehension Application
Tables such as these can be helpful before, during, and after reading a selection. Students can set up a simple K-W-L table, a beginning-middle-end table, or a simple sequence table.

	B	M	E

Storage Notes Set up Vocabulary or Spelling Word binders in workstations so that students have easy access to them.

Folded Tables and Charts Directions
by Dinah Zike

Materials:
• one 11″ × 17″ sheet of paper

Directions:

1. Fold the number of vertical columns needed to make the table (or chart).

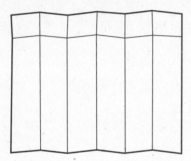

2. Fold the horizontal rows needed to make the table. (If you use loose-leaf paper, you may not need to do this step.)

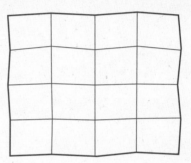

Use this Foldable to _____

_____

_____

_____

_____

_____

_____

Foldables

Correlated to Reading Skills

Foldable	Phonics/Spelling	Vocabulary	Vocabulary Strategies	Comprehension	Study Skills	Grammar
Accordion Book		X	X	X		X
Standing Cube		X		X		X
Large Word Study Book	X	X				
Layered Book	X	X		X	X	X
Four-Door				X		X
Two- and Three-Tab	X			X		
Four- and Eight-Tab	X	X		X		
Matchbook and Portfolio	X	X		X	X	
Shutter				X		
Pyramid	X	X		X		
Two- or Three-Pocket	X	X		X		
Folded Tables and Charts	X	X	X	X		

Learn More About Foldables™

Dinah Zike is the author of more than 150 educational books and materials. For a catalog of Dinah's current publications, as well as information on her keynotes and teacher workshops, call 1-800-99DINAH (1-800-993-4624), or visit her Web site at www.dinah.com.

Look for *Dinah Zike's Big Book of Phonics, Vocabulary, and Spelling* with 260 full-color pages of Foldable activities and word lists for the K–6 classroom.

Look for other practical and inexpensive storage, display, and organization ideas in *Dinah Zike's Classroom Organization: It Can Be Done.* This newly revised and updated publication is perfect for the K–6 classroom teacher who needs to get organized.

Word Study

Use the pages in this section to offer further practice
with phonics, spelling, and word meanings.

- reproducible cards for each week's words
- tested, review, and challenge words

- reproducible cards for each week's tested words
- blank cards for additional words

- *Learning with Games* – suggestions for games that
  support word study strategies, dictionary skills, and
  comprehension skills
- boards, grids, spinners, and other ideas to customize
  for your class

oddball	flat	cash
bell	grim	wealth
build	left	dock
blot	odd	sum
hint	mill	past
shelf	plot	crunch
plum	band	heavy
shovel	bluff	snack
step	pond	

oddball	pale	face
crate	clay	stray
cane	slate	today
bail	rail	break
ache	drain	faint
flame	claim	steak
neigh	mane	graze
neighbor	railway	plum
grim	cash	

© Macmillan/McGraw-Hill

beam	tea	chief
squeak	peep	weep
sleek	heal	tease
thief	deal	please
leak	league	reef
deed	feet	breathe
speech	wheeze	freedom
appeal	pale	bail
neigh		

© Macmillan/McGraw-Hill

drive	file	kite
wipe	pride	pry
shy	prime	slight
climb	sly	sigh
fright	inside	pies
die	spy	minding
twice	height	highway
wildlife	sleek	please
chief		

chose	own	stove
stone	fold	goal
blown	bolt	toll
flow	mole	mold
lower	sole	groan
quote	stole	foam
mows	coaster	motor
roasting	kite	shy
climb		

Spelling Word Cards

chopped	kitchen	cheap
patch	latch	hitch
arch	ketchup	marching
choose	chef	chant
chatter	snatch	sketched
stretching	pitcher	branch
chance	touch	chemical
checkers	goal	stove
mows		

© Macmillan/McGraw-Hill

phrase	graph	brush
these	nowhere	headphone
shed	whole	photo
washer	rush	northern
thanks	bother	fifth
shove	whisk	thirty
whirl	width	theater
wherever	ketchup	cheap
arch		

shred	through	sprout
sprawl	split	throb
throat	shrink	screw
shrimp	screech	straighten
sprang	shriek	splashing
straps	strain	strand
script	thrill	threaten
strictly	brush	graph
these		

oddball	ford	spark
charge	morning	guard
smart	worn	core
door	bore	dart
award	carpet	cord
fort	argue	ward
barnyard	warp	charcoal
forecast	stormy	throat
shrimp	screech	

oddball	scare	gear
compare	hear	stair
airfare	snare	rear
spare	yearly	fear
beard	appear	area
cheer	tear	mere
spear	lair	career
sincere	staircase	dart
fort	worn	

© Macmillan/McGraw-Hill

birth	worse	pearl
curl	dirty	hurl
swirl	curb	herb
curve	turnip	purpose
purse	blurred	shirt
person	sternly	serpent
turkey	twirl	spurt
further	spare	hear
lair		

Spelling Word Cards

doubt	lambs	honor
wriggle	heir	hour
knew	knives	honest
wrinkle	thumbs	combs
plumber	knead	wrapper
kneel	honesty	known
answer	wrench	knuckles
wrestle	curl	shirt
pearl		

arrange	badge	circus
certain	glance	cement
center	dance	wedge
strange	germs	ginger
bridge	orange	ounce
police	once	spice
sponge	village	general
ceremony	wrench	kneel
combs		

mosses	arches	babies
armies	berries	caves
clams	arrows	dresses
engines	glasses	couches
hobbies	enemies	mistakes
props	parents	patches
mints	ranches	batteries
compasses	germs	spice
circus		

backyard	bedspread	bedroom
campfire	clothesline	desktop
fishbowl	grandparent	blindfold
lookout	loudspeaker	overdo
overhead	bookcase	railroad
newborn	snowstorm	undertake
waterproof	yourself	eyesight
paperweight	arches	dresses
berries		

Spelling Word Cards

ripped	ripping	cared
caring	flipped	flipping
flagged	flagging	forced
forcing	tapped	tapping
tasted	tasting	skipped
skipping	saved	saving
discussed	discussing	outwitted
underscoring	desktop	snowstorm
bedspread		

pennies	cozily	lazier
replied	worried	marries
carries	easily	silliest
cries	prettily	happiest
emptier	sorriest	families
merrier	dizziest	funnier
jumpier	varied	handily
factories	skipped	caring
tasting		

oddball	should	zoom
tunes	brooks	you'll
wool	mood	suits
crew	spool	stool
cookie	food	used
grew	group	stoop
move	stew	huge
crooked	juicy	funnier
pennies	prettily	

oddball	pouch	noises
flower	south	cowboy
gown	mound	frown
pound	voices	voyage
annoy	hound	grown
grouch	howling	cough
wound	thousand	tower
drought	downtown	zoom
cookie	huge	

Spelling Word Cards

© Macmillan/McGraw-Hill

oddball	walker	chalk
laws	stalk	bald
caught	drawn	halt
strawberry	fought	caller
half	straw	small
thought	talking	awe
shawl	false	squall
wallpaper	awkward	south
annoy	pouch	

© Macmillan/McGraw-Hill

thriller	fossil	planner
swallow	member	willow
nodded	foggy	dipper
summer	slender	picket
blossom	ticket	welcome
blanket	plastic	dinner
market	witness	cupboard
friendly	drawn	talking
shawl		

Spelling Word Cards

radar	cabin	habit
never	pity	limit
cider	stolen	razor
wiper	easel	talent
diver	finish	river
bison	level	spoken
promise	famous	sequence
vivid	plastic	swallow
rumbles		

above	cancel	remind
gather	between	unfold
tender	action	monster
chamber	petal	woman
weeder	frosty	clipper
tutor	poster	behave
relate	excite	another
remember	diver	finish
spoken		

barber	zipper	daughter
powder	odor	enter
anchor	tanker	cheddar
grocer	popular	pepper
collar	danger	singer
elevator	harbor	polar
victor	grader	conductor
waiter	tender	behave
cancel		

oddball	medal	local
pebble	special	turtle
bugle	channel	settle
pedal	pupil	pencil
docile	oral	vessel
ankle	bubble	symbol
uncle	paddle	total
animal	snorkel	barber
cheddar	anchor	

bacon	woven	ridden
cannon	common	cotton
cousin	robin	eleven
penguin	muffin	proven
raisin	reason	skeleton
button	often	widen
sunken	wooden	violin
vitamin	paddle	pupil
medal		

doe	dough	bolder
boulder	route	root
patience	patients	moose
mousse	prince	prints
who's	whose	wade
weighed	weave	we've
tail	tale	strait
straight	cotton	eleven
muffin		

discourage	disappoint	disbelief
distrust	disloyal	misplace
mislabel	mislead	misstep
misnumber	nonfat	nonfiction
nonsense	nonstop	unable
unplug	uncertain	uncomfortable
uncover	unclean	mishap
unravel	prince	weighed
bolder		

© Macmillan/McGraw-Hill

aimless	barely	breathless
hopefully	sickness	spotless
illness	furry	goodness
hairy	handful	happiness
tasteless	joyfully	lifeless
purely	certainly	really
sorrowful	sunny	superbly
successful	nonfat	misnumber
disappoint		

Spelling Word Cards

service	alert	modern
concert	eastern	furnace
disturb	merchant	concern
burrow	perhaps	lantern
surprise	purchase	nervous
whirlwind	capture	thirsty
survive	persuade	survey
emerge	really	handful
goodness		

accuse	consume
allergies	evidence
assignments	suspicious
consideration	

Vocabulary Word Cards

climate	shimmer
eerie	silken
lumbering	swallows
lurk	

completed	roamed
journey	wildlife
natural	

astronaut	realistic
endless	sensible
paralyzed	universe
protested	

cluttered	nuzzle
disgusted	raft
downstream	scattered

Vocabulary Word Cards

flinched	**legendary**
fluke	**muttered**
gaped	**snickering**
insult	

© Macmillan/McGraw-Hill

border	overheard
boycotts	strikes
citizen	unions
opportunities	

Vocabulary Word Cards

dynasties	**preserve**
heritage	**temples**
overjoyed	

convinced	independence
dizzy	mischief
handy	nowadays
hilarious	whirlwind

ambulance	harmless
apologize	slithered
cardboard	weekdays
genuine	

agile	interfere
awkward	proclaimed
guardian	tottered

ancestors	**segregation**
avoided	**unfair**
injustice	**unsuspecting**
numerous	

enterprising	persistence
identified	venture

amazement	patchwork
loosened	responsibility
midst	sores
mysterious	

blizzard	magnify
evaporate	microscope
foolishness	negatives
inspire	technique

Vocabulary Word Cards

appreciated	misunderstood
bluffing	neglected
desperate	obedience
endured	risks

cautiously	faint
crisscrossed	jealousy
disguised	wisdom
fade	

decayed	fuels
electrical	globe

dove	snoring
massive	tangles
politicians	unique
rumbling	

Vocabulary Word Cards

brittle	partnership
coral	reef
current	suburbs
eventually	

advanced	positive
consisted	selecting
peculiar	snuffled

Vocabulary Word Cards

bumbling	famished
commotion	selfish
cranky	specialty
exasperated	

documenting	valuable
estimated	vessels
period	

Vocabulary Word Cards

barbecue	skyscrapers
collage	strutting
flicked	swarms
glorious	

coaxing	habitat
descendants	sanctuary
fragile	threatened
glistening	

annoyed	outstretched
disappointment	prospectors
circular	reference
glinted	

acquaintance	scornfully
eavesdropping	scuffling
jumble	wistfully
logical	

fossil	paleontologist
inspected	stumbled upon

applauded	hoisting
assured	unstable
glider	wingspan
headlines	

astronomer	overcome
communication	prehistoric
investigates	solitary
nutrients	territory

Learning with Games

Root Word Find

Materials

Puzzle Pieces, three pieces (p. 138)
Vocabulary Word Cards (pp. 96–125)
pencils

Skill: word parts

Prepare: Give players several copies of the three-part puzzle pieces. Have students write each of their vocabulary words onto the puzzle pieces, dividing the words into the appropriate word parts.

Play: Players name the root words, prefixes, suffixes, and/or endings of each word. Call on them or have them quiz each other in small groups.

If there is time, have players exchange their puzzle pieces with a partner. Have the partner sort the puzzle pieces and put them together to recreate the vocabulary words.

Long Vowel Slip Strips

Materials

Slip Strips or Word Wheel (p. 137, p. 132)
pencils

Skill: build words with long vowel sounds

Prepare: Give each player a copy of the slip strips. Have students write *ay* on the rectangular box to the right of the opening.

Play: Invite players to come up with a variety of words that use the long vowel sound of *ay*. On the slip with four squares, have players write consonants and consonant blends that complete a word. (Players could also use the Word Wheel with *ay* on the outside wheel and consonants and consonant blends on the inside wheel.)

The Suffix Trail

Materials

S-shaped board (p. 131)
4-part spinner (p. 129)
Spelling or Vocabulary Word Cards (pp. 66–125)
pencils

Skill: suffixes

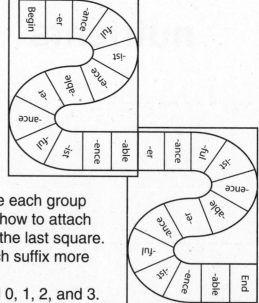

Prepare: This game is for three or four players. Give each group two copies of the S-shaped game board. Show them how to attach the copies. Write *begin* in the first square and *end* in the last square. Then fill the remaining squares with suffixes. Use each suffix more than once.

Each group also needs a 4-part spinner numbered 0, 1, 2, and 3.

Play: Players spin the spinner then move that number of spaces. Then the player must say a word that has the suffix shown. Players may refer to the Spelling or Vocabulary Word Cards. The game ends when a player reaches the *end* square.

Match!

Materials
    Cards (p. 133)
    pencils

Skill: homophones

Prepare: This game is for two players.
Give each pair four copies of the cards.
Have partners write homophones on the
cards. They may use the following words:
*would, wood; right, write; flour, flower;
know, no; passed, past; here, hear; seam,
seem; weak, week; maid, made; fined, find;
scent, cent; patience, patients; see, sea;
ate, eight; meat, meet.*

Play: Begin by dealing ten cards to
each player. Each player looks for any
homophone matches and places them on
the table. Then players take turns asking
each other if they hold the match to one
of their own cards. A player draws from
the remaining cards if the opposing player
cannot give the requested homonym. The
player who ends up with the most matches
is the winner.

Four Corners

Materials
    Tic-Tac-Toe grid (p. 134)
    pencils
    game markers

Skill: contractions

Prepare: Give each player a copy of the
Tic-Tac-Toe grid. Have the players write
a different contraction in each corner. You
may want to write the following contractions
on the board for reference: *won't, I've,
wasn't, it's, doesn't, haven't, isn't, you'll,
aren't, you've, let's, we're, that's, don't,
couldn't, wouldn't, he's, she's.*

Play: Call out the two words that make the
different contractions. Have players place
a marker on the correct contraction. For
example, if you call out *will + not,* the players
place a marker on *won't.* The winner is the
first player to place a marker in each of the
four corners of the Tic-Tac-Toe grid.

Games

Look It Up!

Materials
4-part spinner (p. 129)
Oval board (p. 130)
Vocabulary Word Cards (pp. 96–125)
dictionary
pencils

Skill: dictionary skills

Prepare: This game is for three or four players. Give each group an oval board, a blank spinner, and a dictionary. On the board, mark one square with a star to indicate the beginning and ending point. Have them fill the other squares with current and review vocabulary words. They may refer to their Vocabulary Words Cards for word suggestions.
Label the spinner 1 *Definition*, 2 *Pronunciation Key*, 3 *Word History*, and 0.

Play: Players spin the spinner and move that number of spaces. (0 = skip turn) The spinner will also tell them what they need to find out about the word they landed on. Players use the dictionary to tell the word's definition, pronunciation key, or history. The winner is the first player to reach the star.

Coin Toss

Materials
4 x 4 or 5 x 5 grid (p. 135, p. 136)
pencil
penny

Skill: fact and opinion

Prepare: This game is for four players. Give each group a copy of the 4 x 4 grid. Have each player write his or her name in the first square of one row.

Play: The object of the game is to be the first player to color in each square in their row. Each player flips a penny. If the coin lands on "heads," then the player tells a fact about the school. The player also colors in a square. If the coin lands on "tails," then the player gives an opinion about the school. Players cannot color in a square if they get tails.

Use the 5 x 5 grid if there are five players in a group. To make the game more advanced, have players offer facts and opinions about stories or topics to complete the game.

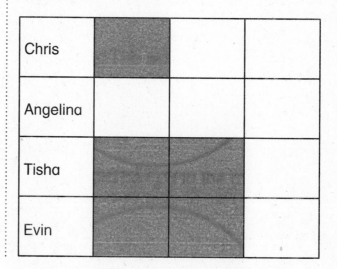

Games

Spinners

1. Cut out and complete a spinner.

2. Mount it on heavy paper.

3. Attach arrow with brad.

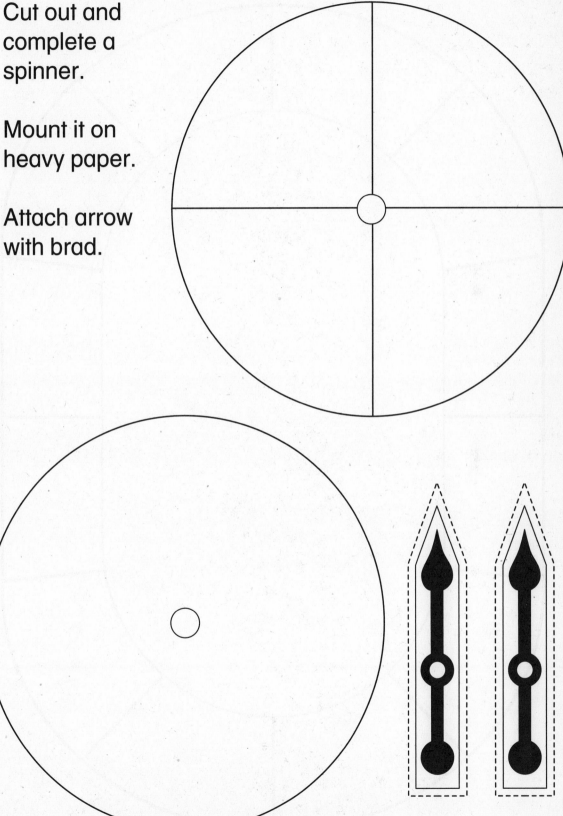

Oval Game Board

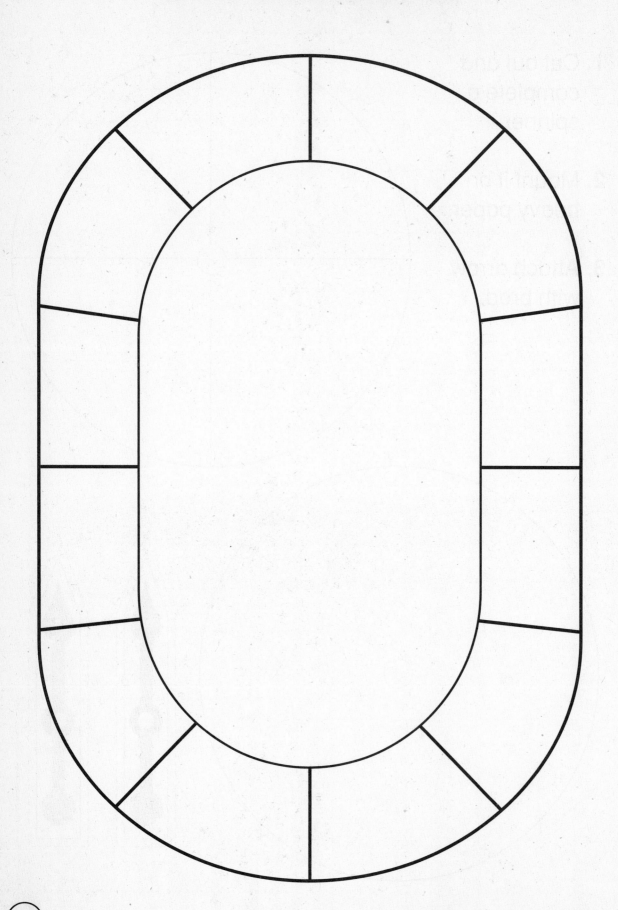

Games

S-shaped Game Board

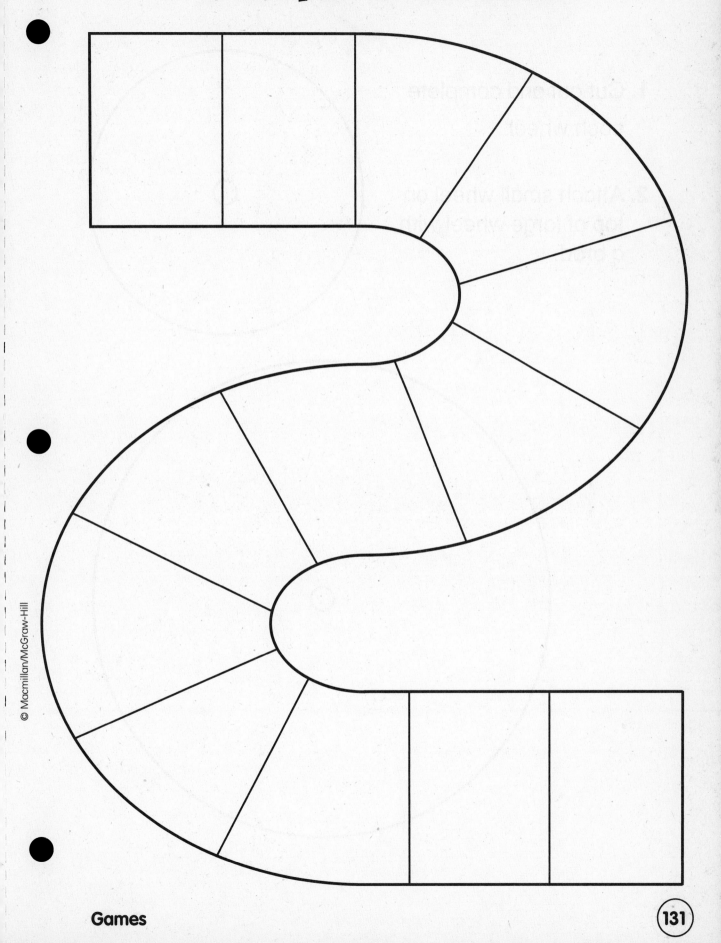

Word Wheel

1. Cut out and complete each wheel.

2. Attach small wheel on top of large wheel with a brad.

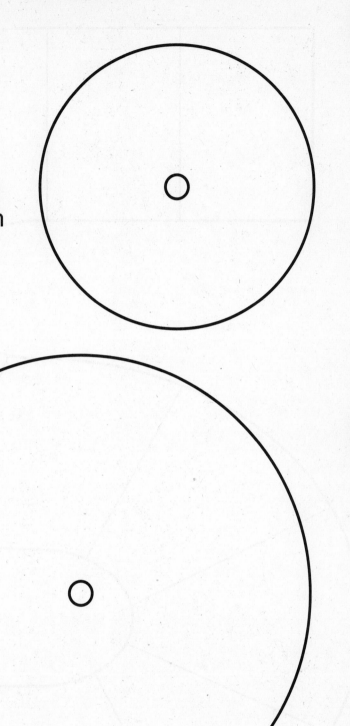

Cards

Games

Tic-Tac-Toe

4x4 Grid

5x5 Grid

Slip Strips

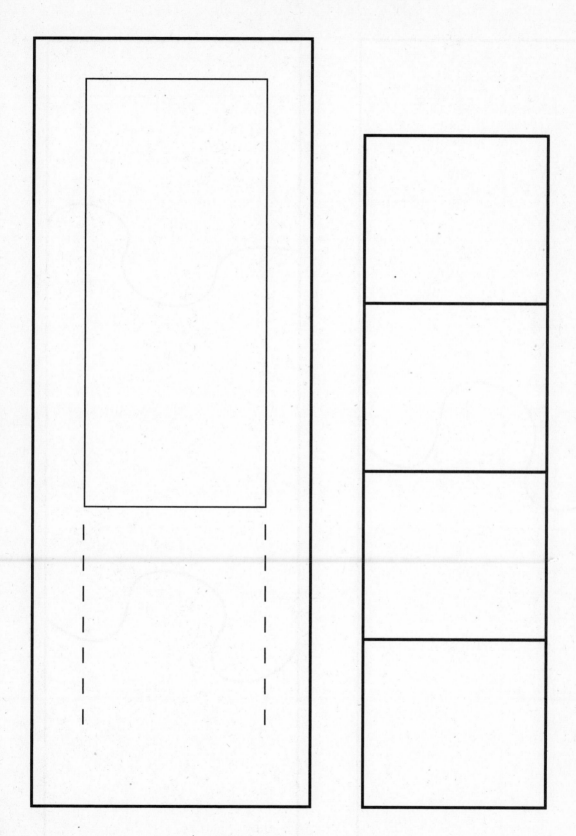

Games

Puzzle Pieces

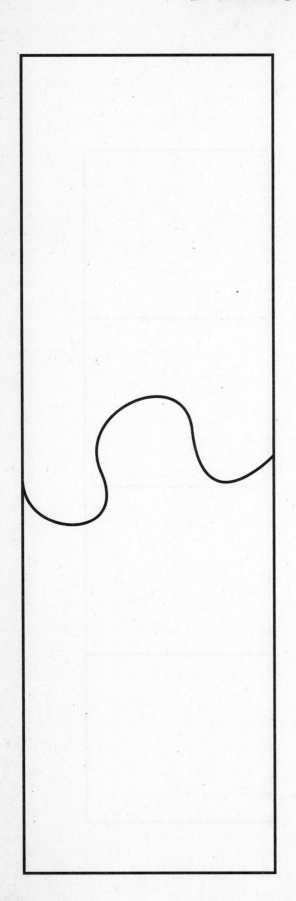

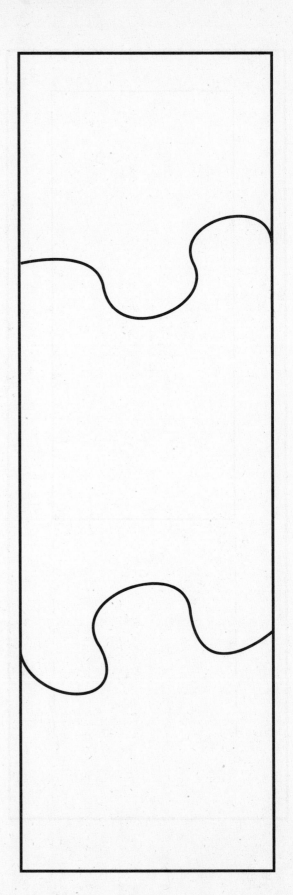

Additional Literacy Support

Use the pages in this section to support reading, writing, handwriting, listening, and speaking activities.

Name _____

Reader Response

Title: _____ Author: _____

Rate this book by coloring in the stars.

Awesome   Good   Okay   Disliked   Disliked a lot

Recommendation: To whom would you recommend this book?

_____

_____

Response: Write one of the following as if it were from the point of view of a particular character.

_____ Poem   _____ One-act play

_____ Song   _____ Journal entry

_____

_____

_____

_____

_____

Reader Response: Fiction

Name _____

Reader Response

Title: _____ Author: _____

Rate this book by coloring in the stars.

Awesome   Good   Okay   Disliked   Disliked a lot

Recommendation: To whom would you recommend this book?

_____

_____

Response: Write a new ending to this story. How will it affect the rest of the story?

_____

_____

_____

_____

_____

_____

_____

Name _____

Reader Response

Title: _____ Author: _____

Rate this book by coloring in the stars.

Awesome   Good   Okay   Disliked   Disliked a lot

Recommendation: To whom would you recommend this book?

_____

Response: What was the most surprising or interesting thing you learned?
Choose one of the following to write your response.

_____ Magazine article   _____ Book review

_____ Letter to a friend   _____ Journal entry

_____

_____

_____

_____

Reader Response: Nonfiction

Name _____

Reader Response

Title: _____ Author: _____

Rate this book by coloring in the stars.

Awesome   Good   Okay   Disliked   Disliked a lot

Recommendation: To whom would you recommend this book?

_____

Response: Write an e-mail to the author describing what you have learned from this book.

To: @example.com
Subject:
Dear_____:
_____
_____
Sincerely,
_____

Name _____

Reader Response

Title: _____ Author: _____

Rate this poem by coloring in the stars.

Awesome   Good   Okay   Disliked   Disliked a lot

Recommendation: To whom would you recommend this poem?

_____

_____

Response: Is this poem like any other poem you have read before? Why?

_____

_____

_____

_____

_____

_____

_____

Reader Response: Poetry

Name _____

Reader Response

Title: _____ Author: _____

Rate this poem by coloring in the stars.

Awesome   Good   Okay   Disliked   Disliked a lot

Recommendation: To whom would you recommend this poem?

_____

Response: Describe how you feel about this poem. What do you like or dislike about this poem?

_____

_____

_____

_____

_____

_____

Name _____

My Writer's Checklist
Personal Narrative

✔ **Put a check by the items you completed.**

☐	Do I write from one of my own personal experiences?
☐	Do I tell how I am feeling?
☐	Do I have a topic sentence that hooks the reader?
☐	Do I use time-order words to show what happened in the beginning, middle, and end?
☐	Do I use words that give details and help create pictures for the reader?

What did I do well in my writing?

1. _____

2. _____

What will I change when I revise this work?

1. _____

2. _____

Teacher: See also Proofreading Marks, page 152, and Writing Rubrics, pages 153–160.

Writer's Checklists

Name _____

My Writer's Checklist
Persuasive Writing

✔ **Put a check by the items you completed.**

☐	Do I state my opinion in the opening paragraph?
☐	Do I give facts and examples to support my opinion?
☐	Do I present my reasons in a logical order?
☐	Do I tell the reader why this issue is important to me?
☐	Do I use opinion words?

What did I do well in my writing?

1. _____

2. _____

What will I change when I revise this work?

1. _____

2. _____

Teacher: See also Proofreading Marks, page 152, and Writing Rubrics, pages 153–160.

My Writer's Checklist

Story

✔ **Put a check by the items you completed.**

☐	Do I focus my story on a main character and problem?
☐	Do I include descriptive details about the main character?
☐	Does my story have a beginning, middle, and end?
☐	Do I tell how the problem is resolved?
☐	Do I use dialogue that sounds natural?

What did I do well in my writing?

1. _____

2. _____

What will I change when I revise this work?

1. _____

2. _____

Teacher: See also Proofreading Marks, page 152, and Writing Rubrics, pages 153–160.

My Writer's Checklist
Explanatory Writing

✔ **Put a check by the items you completed.**

☐	Do I explain all the steps a reader would need to carry out the task or project?
☐	Do I start with a topic sentence?
☐	Do I present the steps in a logical order?
☐	Do I show enthusiasm in my writing?
☐	Do I use time-order or spatial words to make the steps clear?

What did I do well in my writing?

1. _____

2. _____

What will I change when I revise this work?

1. _____

2. _____

Teacher: See also Proofreading Marks, page 152, and Writing Rubrics, pages 153–160.

Name _____

My Writer's Checklist
Compare and Contrast Essay

✔ **Put a check by the items you completed.**

☐	Do I introduce two items to compare?
☐	Do I tell how the items are alike and different in each paragraph?
☐	Do I present the details in logical order?
☐	Do I summarize my most important points in the conclusion?
☐	Do I use a variety of compare and contrast words?

What did I do well in my writing?

1. _____

2. _____

What will I change when I revise this work?

1. _____

2. _____

Teacher: See also Proofreading Marks, page 152, and Writing Rubrics, pages 153–160.

My Writer's Checklist

Research Report

✔ Put a check by the items you completed.

☐	Do I clearly state my main idea?
☐	Do I provide facts and details to explain my main idea?
☐	Do I draw a conclusion at the end?
☐	Do I use transition words to help connect ideas?
☐	Do I vary sentence types and lengths?

What did I do well in my writing?

1. _____

2. _____

What will I change when I revise this work?

1. _____

2. _____

Teacher: See also Proofreading Marks, page 152, and Writing Rubrics, pages 153–160.

Proofreading Marks

☰	Make a capital letter.	we went to the park.
/	Make a small letter.	We walked by the Lake.
⊙	Add a period.	The fish were jumping⊙
⌄̬	Add a comma.	I saw ants͜frogs, and a bird.
⌄ ⌄	Add quotation marks.	⌄What time is it?⌄asked Mom.
⌄	Add an apostrophe.	Dan's watch was broken.
ⓢⓟ	Check spelling.	The sky was (beuatiful) ⓢⓟ
∧	Add.	Then∧ate lunch. *we*
℘	Take out.	The tall trees were very tall.
¶	New paragraph	¶ The town seemed busy and noisy after our day at the park.

Proofreading Marks

Writing Rubric

4 Excellent	3 Good	2 Fair	1 Unsatisfactory
• tells about a personal experience and includes thoughts and feelings	• tells about a personal experience and includes some thoughts and feelings	• tells about a personal experience but loses focus	• does not share a personal experience
• includes a strong beginning and end	• presents details in the correct order	• includes events that are told out of order	• tells events out of order and is confusing
• brings across a strong personal message	• makes an effort to share a message	• shows little personal involvement	• does not express feelings or connect with readers
• uses a variety of words in a natural way	• uses appropriate words	• does not use descriptive words or uses words poorly	• uses words not connected to the purpose
• uses a variety of sentences that flow	• uses a variety of complete sentences	• uses only simple sentences	• uses run-on sentences and sentence fragments
• is free or almost free of errors	• has minor errors that do not confuse the reader	• makes frequent errors that confuse the reader	• makes serious and repeated errors
• is easy to read and free of word processing or handwriting distractions	• is mostly easy to read and mostly free of word processing or handwriting distractions	• is readable, but handwriting or word processing errors are distracting	• is difficult to read because of word processing or handwriting errors

Writing Rubric

	4 Excellent	3 Good	2 Fair	1 Unsatisfactory
	• presents a clear opinion with supporting details	• presents a clear opinion with supporting details	• attempts to present an opinion but supporting details are weak	• does not present an opinion
	• presents reasons in a logical order	• presents reasons for an opinion in a logical order	• presents reasons for the opinion, but not in a logical order	• is poorly organized, with disconnected ideas
	• shows strong interest in the issue and connects to readers	• shows interest in the issue and connects to readers	• shows little connection with readers	• is dull and unconvincing
	• uses opinion words and other well-chosen words	• uses opinion words	• uses only one or two opinion words	• uses words not appropriate for the purpose
	• uses sentences that flow	• uses a variety of sentence types	• is choppy and awkward	• uses incomplete sentences
	• is free or almost free of errors	• has minor errors that do not confuse the reader	• makes frequent errors that confuse the reader	• makes serious and repeated errors
	• is easy to read and free of word processing or handwriting distractions	• is mostly easy to read and mostly free of word processing or handwriting distractions	• is readable, but handwriting or word processing errors are distracting	• is difficult to read because of word processing or handwriting errors

Writing Rubric

	4 Excellent	3 Good	2 Fair	1 Unsatisfactory
	• creates an entertaining, detailed story	• creates a solid, detailed story	• attempts to create a story with some details	• does not tell a story
	• moves readers through an engaging beginning, middle, and end	• creates a clear beginning, middle, and end	• has an unclear beginning, middle, and end	• does not have a beginning, middle, and end
	• uses an original voice with well-crafted dialogue	• attempts to create a personal style	• lacks involvement with readers	• shows no engagement with readers
	• uses advanced words and figurative language	• uses both new and everyday words	• uses words that are unclear with no figurative language	• uses words that are either incorrect or do not fit with the story
	• includes a variety of sentences that flow	• includes easy-to-follow sentences	• includes sentences that are understandable but awkward	• uses incomplete or confusing sentences
	• is free or almost free of errors	• has minor errors that do not confuse the reader	• makes frequent errors that confuse the reader	• makes serious and repeated errors
	• is easy to read and free of word processing or handwriting distractions	• is mostly easy to read and mostly free of word processing or handwriting distractions	• is readable, but handwriting or word processing errors are distracting	• is difficult to read because of word processing or handwriting errors

Writing Rubric

4 Excellent	3 Good	2 Fair	1 Unsatisfactory
• creates a focused explanation with clear details	• creates a solid explanation with clear details	• tries to explain, but details may be unclear	• creates an incomplete explanation
• explains the task in an engaging way, with steps presented in a logical order	• introduces the topic and presents steps in a logical order	• presents some steps out of order	• does not include a clear beginning and steps are not presented in order
• uses a personal style and shows an original knowledge of the task	• uses a personal tone and shows knowledge	• does not connect to readers with enthusiasm	• does not use a personal voice and shows little knowledge of the topic
• uses time-order words and precise verbs	• includes some time-order words and some precise verbs	• includes few time-order words and uses unclear verbs	• uses words that do not explain the task, with no time-order words
• uses a variety of sentences that flow	• includes varied easy-to-follow sentences	• includes readable sentences, but sentences lack variety	• includes incomplete and confusing sentences
• is free or almost free of errors	• has minor errors that do not confuse the reader	• makes frequent errors that confuse the reader	• makes serious and repeated errors
• is easy to read and free of word processing or handwriting distractions	• is mostly easy to read and mostly free of word processing or handwriting distractions	• is readable, but handwriting or word processing errors are distracting	• is difficult to read because of word processing or handwriting errors

Writing Rubric

	4 Excellent	3 Good	2 Fair	1 Unsatisfactory
	• compares and contrasts two items or topics, with supporting details	• compares and contrasts two items or topics	• makes an unclear comparison with few details	• does not make a comparison of two items or topics
	• arranges ideas logically, with good transitions	• organizes the comparison well with transitions	• does not identify the topic and puts details out of order	• has no organization or flow
	• shows detailed knowledge about the subject and speaks to readers	• uses an informative tone	• does not connect well with readers and shows incomplete knowledge	• does not connect with readers and shows little or no knowledge
	• uses precise compare and contrast words	• uses compare and contrast words correctly	• uses few compare or contrast words	• uses only general words or words that do not provide meaning
	• uses sentences in which ideas flow smoothly	• uses easy-to-follow sentences	• uses choppy sentences	• includes incomplete and confusing sentences
	• is free or almost free of errors	• has minor errors that do not confuse the reader	• makes frequent errors that confuse the reader	• makes serious and repeated errors
	• is easy to read and free of word processing or handwriting distractions	• is mostly easy to read and mostly free of word processing or handwriting distractions	• is readable, but handwriting or word processing errors are distracting	• is difficult to read because of word processing or handwriting errors

Writing Rubric

	4 Excellent	**3 Good**	**2 Fair**	**1 Unsatisfactory**
	• uses well-researched information to state a main idea	• supports a main idea with solid research	• presents limited research and has no main idea	• does not include research or provide facts about the topic
	• includes a strong introduction and conclusion	• has a logical flow of facts and details that support the main idea	• has a weak introduction and conclusion	• is structured poorly and has no conclusion
	• encourages readers' interest and shows knowledge of topic	• has a personal tone and shows knowledge of the topic	• is not fully engaged in the topic and lacks a personal view	• shows little understanding of topic with no personal style
	• uses transition words and accurate vocabulary	• uses words specific to the topic and includes transition words	• chooses poor words for topic and includes few transition words	• uses only basic vocabulary and does not use transition words
	• has sentences that flow and guide readers	• uses a variety of easy-to-follow sentences	• includes choppy and awkward sentences	• includes incomplete and confusing sentences
	• is free or almost free of errors	• has minor errors that do not confuse the reader	• makes frequent errors that confuse the reader	• makes serious and repeated errors
	• is easy to read and free of word processing or handwriting distractions	• is mostly easy to read and mostly free of word processing or handwriting distractions	• is readable, but handwriting or word processing errors are distracting	• is difficult to read because of word processing or handwriting errors

Writing Rubric

4 Excellent	3 Good	2 Fair	1 Unsatisfactory
• Ideas and Content	• Ideas and Content	• Ideas and Content	• Ideas and Content
• Organization	• Organization	• Organization	• Organization
• Voice	• Voice	• Voice	• Voice
• Word Choice	• Word Choice	• Word Choice	• Word Choice
• Sentence Fluency	• Sentence Fluency	• Sentence Fluency	• Sentence Fluency
• Conventions	• Conventions	• Conventions	• Conventions
• Presentation	• Presentation	• Presentation	• Presentation

Writing Rubrics

Writing Rubric

4 Excellent	3 Good	2 Fair	1 Unsatisfactory

Writing to a Picture Prompt

Students are sometimes asked to write about a picture instead of just responding to a writing prompt. The student will either tell about what they see in the picture, or write about something related to the picture. The form of the writing is usually a story or an essay.

Use the picture prompts as additional writing practice or to help students prepare for writing tasks on standardized tests.

Instruct students to do the following:

Before Writing

1. Look closely at the picture. Think about what is happening in the picture.
2. Ask yourself questions about the picture:
   - Where and when are the events shown in the picture taking place?
   - Who or what is in the picture? What are they doing?
   - Can you tell what is happening? What event may have happened prior to this one? What do you think might happen next?
3. You can use a graphic organizer to organize your ideas before you begin to write. You can also make an outline, create an idea web, or do other prewriting work.

During Writing

Use a graphic organizer, or other prewriting work, to write about what is happening in the picture.

After Writing

1. Use the Writer's Checklists, pages 146–151, to help you check your writing.
2. Proofread your writing using Proofreading Marks, page 152.

Name _____

Write to a picture prompt. Look at the photograph below. What National Park would you like to visit? Write a story about a visit to a National Park and what you might see there.

 Writing Tips

- Use a graphic organizer to organize your thoughts.
- Write your story on lined paper.
- Proofread your story.

Write to a picture prompt. Use the picture below. People travel all over the world. Where would you like to travel? Write a story about it.

 Writing Tips

- Use a graphic organizer to organize your thoughts.
- Write your story on lined paper.
- Proofread your story.

Name _____

Write to a picture prompt. The picture shows a community garden. Suppose you decided to help your community. Write a story about how you would help and what might happen.

 Writing Tips

- Use a graphic organizer to organize your thoughts.
- Write your story on lined paper.
- Proofread your story.

Write to a picture prompt. Look at the photograph below. What are some sources of energy you use in your life? Write a story about what might happen if one source of energy were not available for a day.

 Writing Tips

- Use a graphic organizer to organize your thoughts.
- Write your story on lined paper.
- Proofread your story.

Write to a picture prompt. Look at the photograph below. Write a story about a place you have explored or would like to explore.

 Writing Tips

- Use a graphic organizer to organize your thoughts.
- Write your story on lined paper.
- Proofread your story.

Name _____

Write to a picture prompt. Use the picture below. What can you learn from studying the natural world? Write an essay about it.

 Writing Tips

• Use a graphic organizer to organize your thoughts.
• Write your essay on lined paper.
• Proofread your essay.

© Macmillan/McGraw-Hill

Handwriting

A Communication Tool

Although computers are available, many tasks require handwriting. Keeping journals, completing forms, taking notes, making shopping or organizational lists, and reading handwriting are practical uses of this skill.

Writing Readiness

Before students begin to write, they need to develop certain fine motor skills. These are examples of warm-up activities:

- Play "Simon Says" using fingers only.
- Sing finger plays such as "Where Is Thumbkin?" and "The Eensie Weensie Spider," or songs that use Signed English or American Sign Language.
- Use mazes that require students to move their writing instruments from left to right.

Determining Handedness

Keys to determining handedness in a student:

- With which hand does the student eat? This hand is likely to become the dominant hand.
- Does the student start coloring with one hand and then switch to the other? This may be due to fatigue or lack of hand preference.
- Does the student cross midline to pick things up? Place items directly in front of the student to see if one hand is preferred.
- Does the student do better with one hand or the other?

The Mechanics of Writing

Desk and Chair

- Chair height should allow feet to rest flat on the floor.
- Desk height should be two inches above the level of the elbows when the student is sitting.

- There should be an inch between the student and the desk.
- The student should sit erect with elbows resting on the desk.
- Models of letters should be on the desk or at eye level.

Paper Position

- Right-handed students should turn the paper so that the lower left-hand of the paper points to the abdomen.
- Left-handed students should turn the paper so that the lower right-hand of the paper points to the abdomen.
- The nondominant hand should anchor the paper near the top so that the paper doesn't slide.
- The student should move the paper up as he or she nears the bottom of the paper. Many students do not think of this.

The Writing Instrument Grasp

The writing instrument must be held in a way that allows for fluid dynamic movement.

Functional Grasp Patterns

- Tripod Grasp With open web space, the writing instrument is held with the tip of the thumb and the index finger and rests against the side of the third finger. The thumb and index finger form a circle.

- **Quadrupod Grasp** With open web space, the writing instrument is held with the tip of the thumb and index finger and rests against the fourth finger. The thumb and index finger form a circle.

Incorrect Grasp Patterns

- **Fisted Grasp** The writing instrument is held in a fisted hand.
- **Pronated Grasp** The writing instrument is held diagonally within the hand with the tips of the thumb and index finger on the writing instrument but with no support from other fingers.

- **Five-Finger Grasp** The writing instrument is held with the tips of all five fingers.
- **Flexed or Hooked Wrist** A flexed or bent wrist is typical with left-handed writers and is also present in some right-handed writers.

Correcting Grasp Patterns

- Have students play counting games with an eye dropper and water.
- Have students pick up small objects with a tweezer.
- Have students pick up small coins using just the thumb and index finger.
- To correct wrist position, have students check their posture and paper placement.

Evaluation Checklist

Functional handwriting is made up of two elements, legibility and functional speed.

Legibility in Writing
Formation and Strokes

- ☑ Do circular shapes close?
- ☑ Are downstrokes parallel?
- ☑ Do circular shapes and downstrokes touch?
- ☑ Are the heights of capital letters equal?
- ☑ Are the heights of lowercase letters equal?
- ☑ Are the lengths of the extenders and descenders the same for all letters?
- ☑ Do cursive letters that finish at the top join the next letter? (*b, o, v, w*)
- ☑ Do cursive letters that finish at the bottom join the next letter? (*a, c, d, e, h, i, k, l, m, n, r, s, t, u, x*)
- ☑ Do cursive letters with descenders join the next letter? (*f, g, j, p, q, y, z*)

- ☑ Is the slant of all letters consistent?
- ☑ Do all letters rest on the line?

Directionality

- ☑ Are letters and words formed from left to right?
- ☑ Are letters and words formed from top to bottom?

Spacing

- ☑ Are the spaces between letters equal?
- ☑ Are the spaces between words equal?
- ☑ Are spaces between sentences equal?
- ☑ Are spaces between paragraphs equal?
- ☑ Are top, bottom, and side margins even?

Speed

The prettiest handwriting is not functional if it takes students too long to complete their work. After introducing students to writing individual letters, add time limits to copying or writing assignments. Check for legibility.

Handwriting Basics

Handwriting Models – Manuscript

A B C D E F G H

I J K L M N O P

Q R S T U V W

X Y Z

a b c d e f g h

i j k l m n o p q

r s t u v w x y z

Handwriting Models – Cursive

A B C D E F G H

I J K L M N O P Q

R S T U V W X Y Z

a b c d e f g h i j

k l m n o p q r s

t u v w x y z

Handwriting Models – Slant

A B C D E F G H I

J K L M N O P Q R

S T U V W X Y Z

a b c d e f g h

i j k l m n o p q

r s t u v w x y z

Handwriting Practice

Good Listening and Speaking Habits

In our classroom we:

- Follow class procedures and rules

- Respect other people's feelings and ideas

- Speak clearly so that others can understand

- Listen to one another thoughtfully

- Take turns speaking

- Do not criticize people because of their ideas

- Ask good questions

- Do our best and encourage others to do their best

- Answer questions thoughtfully

- Work collaboratively in small groups so that everyone can learn

Classroom Behavior Checklist